European Porcelain

European Porcelain

Mina Bacci

Paul Hamlyn

LONDON · NEW YORK · SYDNEY · TORONTO

Translated by Adeline Hartcup from the Italian original

Le Porcellane Europee

© *1966 Fratelli Fabbri Editori, Milan*

This edition © 1969
The Hamlyn Publishing Group Limited
Hamlyn House,
The Centre, Feltham,
Middlesex

Text filmset in Great Britain by Keyspools Ltd,
Golborne

Printed in Italy by Fratelli Fabbri Editori,
Milan

The passion for porcelain affected the whole of Europe during the 18th century. It was important in the history of taste and fashion, in economic terms and in the related field of industrial development linked with these, and above all it opened up a totally new field in the arts which for a period proved one of the most absorbing.

The decoration and form of porcelain products contained in their essence the subtlest moods of 18th-century art, from the *chinoiserie* of the first period —stimulated by the craze for exotic things which flooded Europe in the late 17th and early 18th centuries, and was inspired by the accounts of travellers and the ever increasing imports of lacquers, porcelain and oriental fabrics—down to the light and flowing forms of 18th-century Rococo.

The new material, luminous and fragile, on which decoration and colour assumed the most remarkable reflections and shades, was one of the mainsprings of the taste, fashion and art of the 18th century. Indeed, the aristocratic society of the day preferred porcelain to work in the precious metals. It is truly incredible how many uses were found for the new material. It was used for decorative articles like plates and vases, for jugs and basins, candlesticks and chandeliers, frames for looking-glasses and clocks, ink-stands and snuffboxes, handles for walking-sticks and cutlery, locks and door-knobs, table-centres of all forms and sizes and whole fireplaces, chess-boards, and tobacco pipes, toilet sets and even bird-cages. A particularly fitting use of the exotic substance was in services for the newly popular beverages, tea, coffee and chocolate, imported to Europe from the Indies and the Orient. Porcelain plaques, mostly with floral designs, were to be found set in all kinds of furniture; statuettes or other decorative subjects, mounted on supports of gilded bronze or *ormolu*, formed frames for clocks and other ornaments. From the earliest years of European porcelain, plates and vases of every shape and size literally lined the walls of the drawingrooms of the wealthy, as for example the one in the Dubsky Palace in Vienna (1725–1735, now partly reconstructed in the Museum of Applied Arts there), the porcelain closet in the castle of Pommersfelden, and the rooms of the 'Japanese palace' and the 'Dutch palace' at Dresden which are known today only from written accounts. The logical conclusion to this development were the 'porcelain rooms' which were a speciality of the Naples factory. In these, whole walls were covered with slabs of porcelain decorated with exotic subjects —while the chandeliers and candlesticks were also of porcelain; a particularly fine example was made for the royal palace at Portici (Plate 51), others being at Aranjuez and at the royal palace at Madrid.

An enormous number of statues and statuettes was also produced. The leading sculptors of the day were not above providing models and sketches; Falconet was actually director of the sculpture department at Sèvres before he went to Russia and Bustelli, from the Ticino, designer at the Nymphenburg factory in Bavaria, can be numbered among the greatest sculptors of 18th-century Europe.

Porcelain is a very hard ceramic, made of a translucent and compact white paste (called the body) with a very high resistance to shocks and heat. The fundamental elements of porcelain are kaolin—a white refractory hydrated aluminium silicate—and feldspars, which form a mixture which can stand very high temperatures (about 1500° C.).

First the article is shaped in the material, after which it is given a preliminary baking in special kilns at about 700°–800° C. This leaves it still partly porous, and it is then coated with a liquid 'glaze' composed of roughly the same substances as the body. It is this glaze which gives the article lustre; the glaze is fused into the body in a second firing at temperatures —as high as 1450°. The kilns are then allowed to cool slowly, and the pieces are taken out to be decorated; this is work for skilled craftsmen working in colours formed from metallic oxides. A third firing at about 800°–900° fixes the decoration, which becomes partially absorbed by the paste. Sometimes decoration is applied after the first firing and before the glaze; this is called 'underglaze' decoration, but only a limited range of colours, the commonest of which is dark blue, can stand the very high temperatures of the

1

1. Medici porcelain, Florence. Oil and vinegar cruet. *c*.1580. Museum für angewandte Kunst, Vienna. The blue decoration on a white ground is typical of Medici porcelain. It derives partly from the traditional design of ancient Tuscan maiolica and partly from the blue and white Ming porcelain which was then becoming known in Europe.

2. Medici porcelain, Florence. Plate. 1575–1587. Victoria and Albert Museum, London. The plate is marked with the cupola of the Duomo at Florence, stylised and with an 'F' in blue. The decoration is derived from oriental designs, particularly the border pattern, with its alternations of stylised flowers, known as 'Chinese clouds'.

3. Rouen. Louis Poterat. Cup and saucer. *c*.1680. Musée des Arts Décoratifs, Paris. Even in the very earliest French soft paste factories, the colour is the blue and white of oriental inspiration. In this case, however, the decoration seems to be inspired by European designs, perhaps from lace or a pattern from contemporary goldsmiths' ware.

4. St Cloud. Pomade jar. Early 18th century. Musée des Arts Décoratifs, Paris. Porcelain was considered especially suitable for containing the creams and pomades which were so much used as cosmetics at that time. Notice the refined oriental stylisation of the form of the large flowers which elegantly cover the surface.

2. Medici porcelain, Florence. Plate. 1575–1587. Victoria and Albert Museum, London.

3. Rouen. Louis Poterat. Cup and saucer. *c.*1680. Musée des Arts Décoratifs, Paris.

4.   St Cloud. Pomade jar. Early 18th century. Musée des
Arts Décoratifs, Paris.

second phase. Unglazed porcelain having a matt surface, is known as 'biscuit'.

European factories evolved two main types of porcelain—'hard paste', white in colour and essentially the same as Chinese porcelain, and 'soft paste', of a milkier colour and particularly important in the history of French porcelain. Kaolin is the essential ingredient of hard paste and the special virtue of kaolin is its plasticity—the Chinese called it the 'bones' of porcelain, and the feldspars the 'flesh'. This plastic quality of the kaolin prevents the article losing its shape and splitting under the strains set up during the firing, when dehydration causes shrinkage. Deposits of kaolin were discovered in Saxony at the beginning of the 18th century, and the German factories, led by Meissen, strove jealously to guard the secret and banned the export of kaolin so that the French industry had to develop a porcelain equivalent without the essential material.

French soft paste, which eventually became commonly known as porcelain, was fired at a lower temperature than hard paste, was less resistant to shocks and heat (though it shared with hard paste its solidity and whiteness) and, as has been said, had a milky tone, differing from the white of hard paste which is always faintly shaded with grey. The glaze for soft porcelain was usually made of a liquid lead enamel. Furthermore, since soft porcelain had to be fired at cooler temperatures, it could take a greater number of colours even though it used metallic oxides like those used for hardpaste decoration; above all it allowed certain shades which were unattainable on hard paste. Indeed it is to soft porcelain that we owe the remarkable colour-range of Sèvres ware, from turquoise to rose Pompadour, from daffodil yellow to grass green.

Attempts to replace the basic substances included the use of a composition known as 'frit', which was made up of ingredients like sand, saltpetre, soda, common salt, chalk and alum. This frit was given a preliminary firing, and was then ground and mixed with clay or chalk. But the mixture was difficult to work with. During the firing process it spoiled and broke easily, so that not more than 20–30% of the work turned out satisfactorily and could be passed on for decoration. The Venice factories and the Coccia works, in particular, employed 'hybrid paste'. This was a paste made of soils containing a small amount of kaolin, as for example the clayey soils of the Tretto, near Vicenza.

The above technical explanations are neither useless nor uninteresting: the problem of porcelain in its early days in Europe was, of necessity, exclusively technical. The production of the very raw material itself involved research on suitable clays, on the most effective mixtures, on the composition of glazes, on minerals suitable for decoration purposes, on the design of kilns, as well as the right temperatures and timing of the different firing phases. The East, where porcelain had been born hundreds of years before, jealously guarded its secrets, and the long tradition of maiolica ware was of no help to Europe, because porcelain presented altogether different problems. The early days of European porcelain were full of hazards. As a consequence of the experimentation with materials, technical considerations, such as the quality and colour of both paste and glaze, are just as important as shape and decoration in determining the origin and date of an article in cases where the marking provides no clue or for some reason remains doubtful.

Porcelain originated in China. Its evolution can most probably be traced back to the 3rd century AD and the first articles in stoneware. This is a compound with a very hard, coloured clay base, half-way between maiolica and porcelain, but the first authentic porcelain seems to have been discovered in the 9th and 10th centuries during the period of the T'ang dynasty. The first European to bring news of these things, 'the loveliest that can be imagined', was Marco Polo, in the 13th century. In his book *Il Milione* he described the city of Tingui, perhaps a district of the province of Che-chiang, and mentioned various pieces which he classified as 'porcelain'. But the term used by the Venetian traveller was not the original one: in China porcelain was called 'Yao', while the word 'porcelain' was used by Western visitors for certain shells which came to be accepted as money. And it must have been a ready metaphor which compared the brilliantly coloured surfaces of the tropical shells with the mysterious material which rivalled the shells in brightness and transparency.

Marco Polo's *Il Milione* was also the source of the many legends which became current in Europe about the composition and virtues of oriental porcelain, legends which were refuted only towards the end of the 17th century when European factories were on the

5.　St Cloud. Jar. *c.*1700. Musée des Arts Décoratifs, Paris.

6.   Meissen. Jar decorated with grasses and waterfowl.
*c.*1725. Staatliche Kunstsammlung, Dresden.

5.　St Cloud. Jar. *c*.1700. Musée des Arts Décoratifs, Paris. The design which adorns the base and shoulders of the jug was to be very popular during the course of the 18th century and is derived from contemporary goldsmiths' ware. The type of decoration recalls that of Plate 3, and may also be inspired by contemporary embroidery.

6.　Meissen. Jar decorated with grasses and waterfowl. *c*.1725. Staatliche Kunstsammlung, Dresden. The border design is of oriental origin; the waterside scene, however, is interpreted with more naturalism and spirit than are similar scenes painted in the East.

7.　Meissen. Style of A. Friedrich von Löwenfink. Vase painted in the Chinese manner. *c*.1730–1735. Porzellansammlung, Dresden. A. F. von Löwenfink was one of the three brothers who played a notable part in the story of the Saxon factory in its early days, working alongside the leading decorator of the time, J. G. Hörold. Until about 1735 the favourite decorative theme was imaginary scenes of Chinese life as seen through European eyes.

8.　Meissen. Johann Joachim Kändler. Statuette known as *The Allegro*. *c*.1740. Staatliche Kunstsammlung, Dresden. Kändler, the leading modeller of the Meissen factory where he worked from 1731 to his death in 1775, was responsible for its finest statuettes.

point of discovering the true composition of porcelain paste. To obtain this paste, according to Marco Polo, the clay had to be kept in the open air for twenty or thirty years, to achieve the material's characteristic colour and remarkable transparency, while a commentator on *Il Milione* believed that porcelain was actually made from sea-shells. A fantastic recipe was offered some three centuries later by Guido Panciroli, an Italian jurist who was a man of many interests. At the end of the 16th century, in his *Brief Account of Certain Excellent Things Known to the Ancients*, he writes that porcelain is 'a substance made of chalk, pounded egg, and shells of sea-locusts, pressed together with other similar things and hidden underground by the maker, who tells none but his children and grandchildren where it is. And they, eighty years later, dig it out and shape it into beautiful vases, adorning it with many different colours . . .'

The scarcity of the articles and the mystery of their composition gave rise to a whole range of beliefs about the magic qualities of porcelain. It was said to ward off certain illnesses and to be a protection against poison, cracking or changing if poisonous substances were poured into it. It is easy to understand how these myths arose. Porcelain is very delicate for everyday use since it takes only the slightest scratch, a mere crack in the surface, to impair the porous foundation. Consequently it was at first reserved for rare use; as for poison, porcelain does in fact change when it comes into contact with caustic alkalis. Thus at the end of the Middle Ages and in the first years of the Renaissance, porcelain was, alongside rock-crystal and 'griffins'

8.   Meissen. Johann Joachim Kändler. Statuette known as *The Allegro. c.*1740. Staatliche Kunstsammlung, Dresden.

eggs' (which were only ostrich eggs), held to have magical powers. Until the 16th century, the rare porcelain objects which found their way from the Far East by way of Arab or Persian travellers, or else across Egypt, the main terminal point of the trade route from Asia to Europe, were exclusively owned by kings and princes, either purchased at fabulous prices or else presented as precious gifts by Eastern princes to European nobles. One of the oldest pieces of Eastern porcelain which reached Europe was the mid 13th-century white vase, with delicate relief decorations, in the Treasury of S. Marco at Venice, which is traditionally believed to have been brought back by Marco Polo himself. '*Plats*', '*pots*' and '*petites écuelles de porcelaine*' are mentioned in the inventories of the Queen of Navarre and the Duke of Anjou (14th century) and in the inventories of the Duke of Berry (early 15th century). Among the richest sources were the sultans of Egypt, who during the 15th century sent frequent gifts of porcelain to the Venetian Doges, to Charles VII of France, whose '*porcelaine de Sinant*' is mentioned by a contemporary source, and to Lorenzo the Magnificent, whose great celadon plate can still be seen in Florence, in the Museo degli Argenti at the Pitti Palace.

The high esteem in which these early pieces of oriental porcelain were held can be seen from the few 15th- and 16th-century paintings in which porcelain objects appear. A good example is Mantegna's *Adoration* (Duke of Northampton's Collection) in which one of the three kings is shown presenting the Christ Child with a small blue and white porcelain

9. Nymphenburg. Francesco Antonio Bustelli. *Pantaloon*. *c.*1760. Bayerisches Nationalmuseum, Munich.

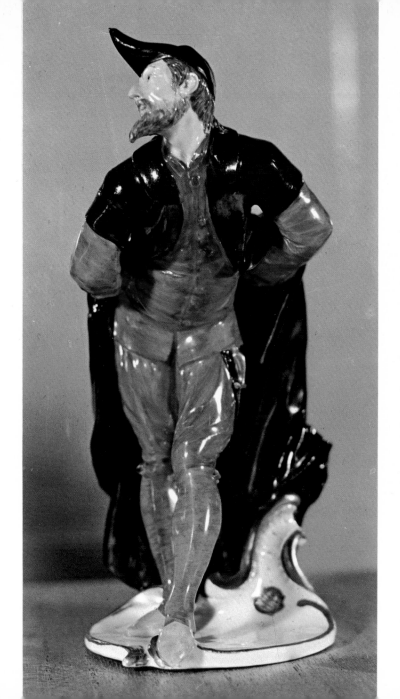

9. Nymphenburg. Francesco Antonio Bustelli. *Pantaloon.* *c.*1760. Bayerisches Nationalmuseum, Munich. This, like the next piece, is a character from the famous set of sixteen figures from the *commedia dell'arte* which Bustelli modelled in the last years of his brief time at the Bavarian factory, from 1754 to 1763. He died, aged just forty, in 1763. The characters of the *commedia dell'arte* were favourites with all European porcelain factories at the time.

10. Nymphenburg. F. A. Bustelli. *Columbine.* *c.*1760. Victoria and Albert Museum, London. This is another of the figures from the popular *commedia dell'arte* series, in which Bustelli succeeded in capturing the personality of the characters, emphasising and bringing out their gestures and emotions. He thus achieved a vivid picture of this important aspect of the life and dress of the European 18th century which was that of the 'improvised comedy' with its buffoonery, comic devices, and humorous and grotesque situations.

11. Chantilly. Ribbed ewer and basin. *c.*1750. Musée des Arts Décoratifs, Paris. Sèvres permitted small French soft paste factories to continue production when they did not represent a dangerous threat to its almost exclusive monopoly. Among these minor factories, the one at Chantilly, founded in 1725 and protected by the Duke de Condé, was one of the most active. Its porcelain never achieved the fine whiteness of Sèvres porcelain, but it has a pleasing and characteristic ivory tone.

10

11. Chantilly. Ribbed ewer and basin. *c.*1750. Musée des Arts Décoratifs, Paris.

cup. Another example is the large dish, also blue and white, which holds the divine nectar in Giovanni Bellini's *Feast of the Gods*, painted in 1514 and now at the Metropolitan Museum, New York. During the 16th century oriental porcelain reached Europe more plentifully after the opening of the route to India round the tip of Africa by Vasco da Gama. Hundreds of thousands of pieces are inventoried in the collections of Francis I of France, Philip II of Spain, the Duke of Bavaria and the Grand Duke of the Tyrol. Spanish galleons raided by English pirates contained much porcelain ware, but they were still rare and curious objects among other valuable merchandise. At the end of the 16th century, oriental porcelain, often mounted in gold or silver by English craftsmen, was a favourite present to Queen Elizabeth from the noblemen of her court. But although these pieces were becoming more widely known, the princes of the period still displayed proudly in their *Kunstkammer* or *Wunderkammer,* their galleries of art and of curiosities.

Meanwhile Europe felt the urge to produce rather than merely import this remarkable material, and from the 16th century onwards trials and experiments were on the increase. One such attempt was 'milk-glass', an opaline substance, made in the first half of the century. Vasari in the second edition of his *Lives*, in the chapter on Academicians of drawing, mentions a 'most excellent teacher, Giulio da Urbino', who worked for Alfonso d'Este at Ferrara. He 'does amazing things with vases made of all sorts of clay, and gets the loveliest effects with the porcelain ones.'

But it is impossible to say today exactly what the 'porcelain' from Ferrara was. The so-called 'Medici porcelain' was, however, very famous, and about forty pieces of this still survive. The experiments promoted by the Grand Duke Francesco I, who was well known for his scientific, or pseudoscientific, interests, were carried out by Bernardo Buontalenti. Vasari calls him a 'man of brilliant talent, who can turn his hand to anything', and especially to 'the speedy manufacture of porcelain vases which have all the perfection of the oldest and finest pieces.' Using the so-called white clay of Vicenza, Buontalenti obtained a yellowish hybrid paste, which had to be covered with a white varnish. The few pieces he made, little flasks of traditional shape derived from contemporary silver, plates, double-spouted vases decorated in blue with floral designs stylised in the Eastern manner, are sometimes imperfect because the glaze has often not taken and the surface is patchy. Only two pieces of Medici porcelain now remain in Florence: a bas-relief portrait of the Grand Duke Francesco I, dated 1586, and a plate with an allegorical figure at its centre. The other pieces are scattered throughout the major European museums (see Plates 1 and 2). Often they were exported soon after they were finished, since the rare pieces which emerged from the Grand Duke's workshop mostly went as gifts to European princes; at the museum at Sèvres, for example, there is a flask bearing the coat-of-arms of Philip II of Spain. After the death of Francesco I in 1587, however, the workshop ceased production.

During the 17th century experiments were carried

out in France. In 1673, Louis Poterat of Rouen obtained from Louis XIV a patent for the manufacture of 'Chinese type' porcelain (Plate 3), while at St Cloud, Pierre Chicaneau made some 'porcelain' pieces which were presented to the court. It is known that other experiments were made at Milan by·Canon Manfredi Settala and in Piedmont by Guidobono, but no pieces survive from these attempts. Articles from the French factories, with blue decoration on a white background, are the first examples of the soft porcelain which played such an important part in the French factories during the 17th century, and which was not altogether abandoned by Sèvres even when, in the later 18th century, it began to produce hard paste.

Meanwhile the early years of the 17th century saw the foundation in Holland, France and England of the three East India Companies for trade with the East. During the century an enormous amount of oriental porcelain poured into Europe, together with other Eastern merchandise which was to raise the passion for *chinoiserie* to fever pitch. In Holland in particular, Eastern ceramics were no longer owned exclusively by princes and kings; the rich burghers also had their collections of oriental porcelain, though these things were still considered refined and precious luxury articles. There is no Dutch still-life painter of the 17th century who did not introduce the blue and white surfaces of porcelain jars, plates and basins into the compositional schemes of sophisticated objects which composed most of the still-life of the time—elegantly shaped amphorae of beaten silver, ostrich-eggs in rich gold and silver settings, Eastern carpets and

12

12.   Vincennes. *The Schoolmistress*. Biscuit. Musée des Arts Décoratifs, Paris. The opacity of biscuit gives a special tenderness to the French factory's figure groups. In place of the animated, grotesque and caricatured subjects of the German factories, the French modellers preferred scenes of love or gentle intimacy.

13.   Sèvres. Cup with lid and saucer. Musée des Arts Décoratifs, Paris. This piece, though dating from the 18th century, is nevertheless distinctly 19th-century both in shape and in its rather static and heavy decoration.

14.   Vincennes. Decorated by J. P. Ledoux. Small souptureen and plate. 1753. Musée des Arts Décoratifs, Paris. A typical French Rococo piece, with handles and the knob on the lid presented in flowing floral terms, while the medallions are outlined in soft gilded sprigs. At Vincennes-Sèvres, where functions were highly specialised, Ledoux painted landscapes and birds.

15.   Sèvres. Jardinière. 1758. Louvre, Paris. This curious form of *cache-pot* freely echoes oriental designs. The fine decoration, again the work of the painter Ledoux, forms an elegant arabesque on the luminous white of the walls.

13. Sèvres. Cup with lid and saucer. Musée des Arts
Décoratifs, Paris.

14. Vincennes. Decorated by J. P. Ledoux. Small soup-
tureen and plate. 1753. Musée des Arts Décoratifs, Paris.

15. Sèvres. Jardinière. 1758. Louvre, Paris.

damasks, fashionable foods like oysters and oranges. However, oriental porcelain is never to be found on the tables of naturalist painters or in the tavern-scenes of a Brouwer or a van Ostade.

It was in fact a Dutchman who finally refuted the legends about the mysterious processes and magic qualities of oriental porcelain. In 1665 Johann Nieuhoff, who towards the middle of the 17th century took part in a mission from the Dutch East India Company to the Emperor of China, published an account of his travels. Passing near the city of Kiotang, writes Nieuhoff, 'the ambassadors, impelled by their eagerness to see such famous and exquisite vases, made their way inside the town. But they found so many people there that they were obliged to turn back discomfited, preferring to retain the respect and veneration due to their rank rather than mingle with the crowds on their way to the shops to satisfy their curiosity.' So there were after all no eye-witnesses to throw light on the subject. Nieuhoff did, however, have the chance of finding things out by talking to local inhabitants, who explained how porcelain was made. The finest porcelain, he was told, was made in a village many miles away, and even there the clay had to be brought from afar, from places where no one knew how to model it. Some people, Nieuhoff adds carefully, consider that the secret lies in the quality of the water and the wood and the temperature of the fire, all of which factors do indeed play a decisive part in the manufacturing process. The clay, the writer continues, is prepared and worked in the same sort of way as the Italians make their faience and the Belgians their white crockery. But the Chinese consider it a major crime to reveal the secret, except to hand on the tradition. And that secret, jealously guarded through the ages, lay in the quality of the clay they used.

A few years later, when the Meissen factory was already completing its first trials after the discovery of suitable clay in the Aue district of Saxony, the word 'kaolin' occurs for the first time in a letter which is entirely concerned with the manufacture of oriental porcelain. This was written in September 1712 by Father d'Entrecolles, a Jesuit missionary in the Kiang-si district, a centre of porcelain production. Meanwhile, as has been indicated, between the end of the 17th century and the first decades of the 18th century, the increasing deliveries of oriental porcelain, especially in Holland, and the more frequent imports of oriental goods, from fabrics to lacquer, caused what amounted to an explosion in the fashion for *chinoiserie* which so greatly influenced 18th-century taste.

Delft pottery, for example, like that of Faenza and Cafaggiolo a century earlier, used decorative themes derived from the Eastern figurative repertory, animals, stylised leaves and flowers painted in blue, while the oriental imagination inspired fantastic scenes in which the figures were given vaguely Chinese features and clothes, and appeared to be engaged in the most strange and extravagant activities. In France, too, during the 17th century, Louis XIV built the little pavilion known as the 'Trianon de Porcelaine' for Madame de Montespan in the royal gardens. This was really a building on Western lines, which was decorated with maiolica in the oriental style but, owing to the fragility of the material used, it fell into ruins a few years later. In France again, at Nevers, the maiolica factories drew widely on the Eastern world for the shapes and above all the decoration of the articles they produced. Thus the 18th century craze for *chinoiserie* was well rooted in the developing taste of the previous century.

Another phenomenon which preceded the discovery of European porcelain by a few years (and which continued for some time until the manufacture of European porcelain was at last established) was the importation into Europe of porcelain goods made in the East for the European market. These articles, services, ornamental plates and statuettes, were known as 'Compagnie des Indes', and are a curious interpretation of the Western world by those who knew it only by hearsay. In their attempts to comply with the taste of Western customers the oriental producers sometimes arrived at truly grotesque effects, which paralleled the equally fantastic interpretations of the lands of the Far East by Western craftsmen. The European decorator applied his art not only to the orientalising of local maiolica wares but also, and here we come to another aspect of the porcelain trade of the early 18th century, to undecorated pieces, which were imported from the East and then painted with stylised oriental designs in European factories, particularly at Meissen.

So we come to the threshold of the discovery of kaolin by Europeans. In the 1670s Walter von Tschirnhaus, a young Bohemian noble who was

16

16.   Sèvres. Decorated by Evans. Bowl from the 'Buffon' service. 1779. Louvre, Paris. The service takes its name from the accurate paintings of animals, which were inspired by the publications of the naturalist, Buffon. The decorator Evans, a specialist in animals, worked at the factory from 1752 to 1806, and signed services like this one.

17.   Orléans. Cup with lid and saucer. Sèvres Museum. The Orléans factory (1753–c.1811) was one of the small soft porcelain factories which Sèvres allowed to carry on. The piece represents a fairly late stage of the 18th century: notice the rigid shape of the handles and the more solid and symmetrical decoration freed from the Rococo style.

18.   Rue du Petit Carrousel. Ewer and Basin. Sèvres Museum. This is a product of one of the small French factories which proliferated and had brief careers in the 18th and 19th centuries. The piece can be dated to the end of the 18th century by its restrained yet elegant shape and decoration.

19.   Sèvres. So-called 'tortoise-shell' plate. 1792. Sèvres Museum. At the end of the 18th century, animals and plants, which in the preceding decades were a pretext for elegant decorative designs, came to be reproduced accurately. This was no doubt due to the new scientific interests of the 18th century, since they were often named in accordance with Linnean nomenclature.

17. Orléans. Cup with lid and saucer. Sèvres Museum.

18. Rue du Petit Carrousel. Ewer and basin. Sèvres Museum.

19. Sèvres. So-called 'tortoise-shell' plate. 1792. Sèvres Museum.

studying at the university of Leyden, was exploring Europe on his 'Grand Tour'. Like many young noblemen of the age he visited many of the courts and capitals. However, Tschirnhaus was no conventional aristocrat dilettante, but a man of remarkable scientific interests. In 1674 he was in London, a year later he was in Paris, where he was in touch with the members of the Académie Royale des Sciences and was embarking on research work on the subject of clay. He was afterwards also at Milan, where, with Manfredi Settala, he carried out experiments on the fusion of clays by means of burning-glasses. He continued his travels throughout Europe in search of patrons for his work, and in 1696 arrived in Saxony where two years before Augustus I, known as Augustus the Strong, had become Elector. Tschirnhaus was soon afterwards in touch with Johann Friedrich Böttger, the Elector's young alchemist, and as a result of their meeting Böttger too joined in the search for the mysterious clay which held the legendary secret of porcelain. At that time such a search must have been as fascinating as the quest for the philosopher's stone, Böttger's true vocation. Their experiments took place at Albrechtsburg, a prison-fortress not far from Dresden, at Meissen, a name which was to become famous in the history of European porcelain. Tschirnhaus died in 1708, and less than a year later Böttger presented the Elector with the first 'porcelain' products. The pieces, some of which still survive, were in fact made of very hard red stoneware, but soon afterwards, with the discovery of kaolin, white porcelain was successfully produced; and in 1710 Augustus established the first European porcelain factory.

The secret material has often been said to have been discovered by chance, and romantic stories have surrounded the unravelling of a problem which in fact took long years of research and exhausting experiments. Certainly the vicissitudes of the first discoveries and the exploits of the first 'arcanists', those who were first entrusted with the secret (Latin, *arcana*), seemed deliberately designed to give free rein to fancy. Even if much was invented or exaggerated to highlight the sensational and mysterious aspects, the element of adventure was certainly not missing from the early days of European porcelain; indeed, as has been said, the spirit in which the research, testings and experiments took place must have been not unlike the all-absorbing mystery of the alchemists' quest. It is hard to say which of the two pioneers, Tschirnhaus or Böttger, deserves the credit for the discovery of porcelain. It was certainly easy for Böttger, after Tschirnhaus's death, to claim the discovery, and indeed Böttger was the one who in modern terms could be described as a first class chemist; but no small part of the credit must go to Augustus of Saxony, who fostered and financed, at great expense, the early discoveries.

The Elector imposed the strictest secrecy on Böttger and all those who knew about the manufacturing processes, enforcing this with threats of the direst punishments, and pretty well holding them prisoners in the Meissen fortress where they conducted their researches. But the secret was soon out. Böttger himself may have played a part, albeit unconsciously, in the disclosure. It appears that just before he died he took to drink, and let out the secret to Konrad Hunger, a Meissen worker. Hunger fled from Saxony and offered his services to a new factory which Innocentius du Paquier had founded in Vienna. But the composition of the paste was not the only secret; the processes of decoration and the methods and times of firing of the new ceramic, presented a range of problems quite different from the traditional techniques of maiolica production. Du Paquier's factory began to function regularly only when another arcanist from Meissen, Samuel Stölzel, went secretly to Vienna. By 1717 Meissen was no longer the only European factory producing the new porcelain. Three years later the restless Hunger, after a disagreement with du Paquier, moved on once again from Vienna to work with a goldsmith in Venice, Francesco Vezzi, who was eager to start a porcelain factory. The kaolin reached the Venetian factory from the deposits in Saxony, and evaded the heavy import taxes. But when the factory began to find itself in troubled waters—the initial costs were gigantic and the whole management was deeply in debt—Hunger went back to Meissen, where he revealed that the kaolin from Aue was being secretly exported to Venice. From that moment strict measures prevented the export of the precious clay and, after an unsuccessful attempt with local material, the first Italian porcelain factory was obliged to close in 1727.

These were the years of the wandering arcanists, who offered their services all over the Continent, where factories making both soft and hard porcelain were on the increase. A few mountebanks who passed

20. Rue de Bondy. Tea-pot. Sèvres Museum.

21. St Petersburg. Small cup with lid. *c.*1830–1840. Musée des Arts Décoratifs. Paris.

20.   Rue de Bondy. Tea-pot. Sèvres Museum. The Rue de Bondy factory (1781–1796) was one of the small works, mostly making hard paste, which multiplied when the Sèvres monopoly was relaxed. In this tea-pot, which bears its owner's initials, as in the other pieces of the service, the traditional decorative themes, flowers, festoons etc., still survive. But from now on they are arranged symmetrically, thus anticipating the Neo-classical style.

21.   St Petersburg. Small cup with lid. c.1830–1840. Musée des Arts Décoratifs, Paris. The attribution to the Russian factory is not certain. The shape of the article is certainly derived from French models. One notices how the shape has grown heavier, and the decoration, dominated by gold against a coloured background, thickened and hardens.

22.   St Petersburg. Tea-pot. Victoria and Albert Museum, London. The piece, evidently part of a service destined for a noble family whose initials it displays, belongs to the time of Catherine II (1762–1796), who did so much to promote the Russian factory. When factories belonged to a king or prince, their products often served as gifts to members of the court or foreign royalty.

22

themselves off as experienced arcanists slipped in among the genuine craftsmen; not for nothing was the 18th century the age of adventurers great and small. Yet even the genuine experts did not know all the secrets of handling the pastes, the length of firing times, and the methods of decoration and, as can be imagined, the impostors succeeded in squandering vast sums for those rash enough to trust them.

Less than fifty years after the first experiments at Meissen, a large number of factories for the manufacture of hard and soft porcelain had started work in Europe. To mention only the most important in chronological order: Vienna, in 1717; Vezzi's factory at Venice; Chantilly; Doccia; Vincennes (later transferred to Sèvres); Capodimonte (transferred to Buen Retiro in Spain, and followed by the royal manufactory at Naples); Bow; Chelsea; Höchst; Berlin; Worcester; Fürstenberg; Le Nove at Bassano; Nymphenburg; Frankenthal; and Ludwigsburg. After 1760 the most important factories founded were a second one at Venice, founded by Geminiano Cozzi, Zürich, the Duke of Angoulême's (after the French Revolution this passed to two 'citizens', Dihl and Guerhard), Vinovo in Piedmont, Copenhagen, Dagoty in France and the factory at St Petersburg which was mainly promoted by Catherine II.

During their early years the first factories did not have much success. The initial costs were enormous, and the first products turned out mostly imperfect as the grey paste was porous, and split or warped during the firing. The arcanists, when they were not downright impostors, boasted special knowledge which they often did not possess, and the public taste was at first not attracted by the new material, preferring the more familiar maiolica. As, however, the passion for porcelain spread, more and more kings and princes vied with each other in giving their help and patronage to existing factories on the verge of bankruptcy, or else founded factories at great expense themselves. The decisive part played by Augustus the Strong in the Meissen factory has already been mentioned. The Capodimonte factory owed its existence to Charles, the Bourbon King of Naples, and his son Ferdinand IV was responsible for reopening the Neapolitan factory. The Copenhagen works were mainly promoted by the Queen of Denmark, and those at St Petersburg by Catherine II of Russia.

In Vienna, du Paquier, at the point of bankruptcy, handed the factory over to the Emperor in 1744. In 1753 Louis XV, on the advice of the Pompadour, gave his protection to the Vincennes factory which took the name of the Manufacture Royale des Porcelaines de France. In Berlin, after the Seven Years War, the porcelain works were taken over by the state. Chantilly was under the protection of the Duke of Condé, Nymphenburg owed its existence to the Duke of Bavaria, and Höchst to the Archbishop Elector of Mainz. Fürstenberg had been founded by Carl I of Brunswick, Ludwigsburg by the Duke Carl Eugen of Württemberg, and the Duke of Angoulême was responsible for the factory which bore his name. Frankenthal, in the Palatinate, was taken over by the Elector Carl Theodor seven years after it was founded by Paul Hannong.

23. Bow. Two candlesticks. London Museum, London.

24. Chelsea. Group depicting one of Aesop's Fables. Menstrie Museum, Bath.

23. Bow. Two candlesticks. London Museum, London. Porcelain was used for innumerable articles during the 18th century. Candlesticks and chandeliers were most often made in porcelain, and sometimes provided a pretext for Arcadian and mythological scenes. In this case the candlesticks represent two figures which evidently belonged to a series dedicated to the seasons, one of those allegories so dear to 18th-century taste.

24. Chelsea. Group depicting one of Aesop's Fables. Menstrie Museum, Bath. The animals of Aesop's fable serve as pretext, together with the rich floral design, for a composition which is full of movement. The Chelsea factory was one of the most important English works making soft paste porcelain.

25. Worcester. Plate. Menstrie Museum, Bath. The Worcester factory developed between 1751 and 1783. The piece shown here dates from about 1770. Typical of the English factory are this midnight-blue decoration, with white medallions framed in a delicately designed Rococo setting, and the masses of vividly coloured flowers.

25

In Italy the Venetian Republic, after Vezzi's unfortunate experiment, gave splendid help and protection to the Venetian factories. At Doccia, the Marquis Carlo Ginori was the enthusiastic and generous founder of the leading Italian porcelain works. The English factories, however, were all due to private enterprise, without aristocratic protection or lavish help from the state, and the same can be said of the Swiss factories at Zürich and Nyon, and those in Holland.

There were many reasons for this multiplication of identical industries. The most obvious motive was ambition: to be the owner or protector of a factory making this new material, which was becoming the great vogue of the century, more highly prized than the traditional treasures, helped to increase the prestige of a ruling house or noble family. Carl Eugen of Württemberg, in the foundation statute of his Ludwigsburg works, declared that the factory was 'indispensable to the splendour and dignity' of his line. But other much more concrete considerations contributed to the expansion of the porcelain industry. The economic theories elaborated in the 17th century by Colbert, France's Controller of Finance, aimed at promoting industries of all kinds as a means of raising the level of economic activity in the country and of developing new sources of ready cash to supplement traditional taxation. At the same time Colbert aimed to prevent currency leaving the country, in this case for the purchase of oriental porcelain. There were also vague social purposes, put forward more or less in good faith, such as the provision of employment.

Certainly in their early years the porcelain works seem to have been an expensive and ambitious caprice and, to begin with at least, they operated at a loss. The Doccia factory, for example, of all those which started through a decision taken by a prince or nobleman, seemed to be directed by an 'enlightened' guidance rather than for a whim or ambition. Yet even Doccia could not sell its first products till 1744, nine years after its foundation, and it was operating at a loss until the death of its founder in 1757.

Added to this was the fact that much of the output from the royal factories was taken up in supplying the needs of the court and in providing gifts. These ranged, according to the importance of the recipient, from simple snuffboxes to dinner services, comprising hundreds of pieces, for official banquets. Sooner or later all the factories opened their sales to the public, often in places adjoining the works. Later, to appeal to the uncultivated public, who did not at first appreciate the new material, travelling salesmen, as can be seen from contemporary engravings, went around offering their new wares from baskets and boxes.

But porcelain was still far from cheap, as must be evident from the very high production costs. It is, however, difficult to compare the prices from the different factories, though we have ample documentation about this, because of the great variety of monetary systems in 18th-century Europe, and it is equally hard to translate the cost of these things into modern prices. For example, in about 1730 the big Meissen vases cost 100 thalers each, and a complete tea or coffee service cost 55 thalers. At Sèvres the vases went from 250 to 600 livres, according to the decoration and mounting. The services, running to hundreds of pieces, fetched fabulous sums—like the one which was given to Queen Catherine II of Russia, which in 1778 reached the price of 328,000 livres. This cannot compare, however, with the prices paid today in the antiquarian market for the most spectacular pieces of porcelain. Bustelli's *commedia dell'arte* figures cost nine florins at the most when they were produced; a few years ago, a group of nine masked figures by Bustelli fetched £36,651 at a London auction.

Because of the high production costs and the relatively small market 18th-century factories resorted to various forms of advertising. Lotteries and auction sales were organised, commercial advertisements appeared in the gazettes of the day or in leaflets to be distributed to the public. The Chelsea factory in England seems to have been in the forefront of this advertising field, for as early as 1755 they were distributing catalogues which listed descriptions and prices of their goods. And more extreme measures were employed which today might not be thought exactly orthodox. Frederick II of Prussia, for example, imposed compulsory purchases of fixed amounts of Berlin porcelain on certain sections of the population, notably the Jews, in exchange for the licences and permits they needed.

As the factories grew in number, they had to protect the reputation of their products from the effects of competition. It was not, however, a matter of safeguarding particular shapes or decorative designs, for ideas circulated freely and swiftly and, as copyright was still unknown, themes taken from sculpture, painting and engravings were common property. The lesser German factories, for example, plagiarised the ideas of Meissen or Vienna, who in their turn went over to the Rococo style from the middle of the 18th century, imitating French shapes and decorating them 'à la Watteau', while the Doccia factory actually traced the design of services from the works at Meissen or Vienna. What factories were protecting was their finished product, and they did this by giving their wares exclusive 'marks' (these are listed later in the chapters on the individual factories). A phenomenon, not at first given much consideration, but which soon became a formidable source of competition for the big factories, particularly the German ones, was the activity of the *Hausmaler*, self-employed or home-based printers. Some of these *Hausmaler* worked in direct association with the factory and their activity grew to vast proportions, particularly in Vienna, but others purchased the undecorated ware and rejects from the works, decorated them and marketed them themselves. The harm caused to a factory by this latter group was not so much that of competition from rival producers marketing the same material, but rather the discrediting of the factory's reputation by the marketing of faulty products, often decorated with colours which would not last. For this reason, from the middle of the 18th century onwards, strict measures were taken to limit the activities of the *Hausmaler*, and faulty pieces, when they were not actually destroyed, were marked with special warning marks.

26

26.   Meissen. Tea-pot. *c*.1740. Victoria and Albert Museum, London. This piece is decorated by a *Hausmaler,* i.e. one of the 'home-based painters' who were particularly important in the German factories for their decorative work. This is often rather coarse, and is taken from the ordinary designs used by the factories.

27.   Doccia. Some pieces from a coffee service. Museo del Castello Sforzesco, Milan. These pieces are typical of the Tuscan factory at the close of the 18th century (particularly the shape of the sugar-bowl). Notice the cylindrical shape of the cup, the framing of the views, the ample room left on the white surfaces.

28.   Naples. Coffee-pot. Museo Principe Pignatelli-d'Aragona, Naples. The shape is derived from early 19th-century French designs. The lavish use of gold reflects the slightly heavy taste which influenced porcelain during the first decades of the 19th century. The scene is in line with academic painting of the period.

In this general discussion of porcelain marks it should be pointed out that they do not offer a fool-proof method of identifying or guaranteeing an article. From the middle of the 19th century, the imitation and forgery of authentic pieces was a busy and evidently lucrative business. The distinction between imitation and forgery is deliberate because often the reproduction of particularly successful traditional models, in those factories which survived the first decades of the 19th century, was not done with any fraudulent intent. Doccia, for example, acquired the models from the Naples works, which were in danger of being lost, and copied them in hard paste, marking them too with the 'N' which was the Naples initial.

More recently copies of famous early designs have been manufactured with no intent at all to deceive, yet it is easy for the amateur to be mistaken as to their age. The Naples pieces, reproduced by Ginori in the 1930s and 1940s, can be distinguished from the originals either by the difference in the colour and consistency of the hard paste, or by their weaker modelling. Deception only occurs when an article is actually passed off as old, and when dates are faked, as has sometimes been the case with Sèvres ware. But apart from cases of particularly clever and accurate forgery, by no means rare, faked pieces give themselves away in various respects—by the paste which is often faulty or too heavy, by colours which are too

27. Doccia. Some pieces from a coffee service. Museo del Castello Sforzesco, Milan.

28. Naples. Coffee-pot. Museo Principe Pignatelli-d'Aragona, Naples.

crude or too pale compared with the original ones, by the gold which is usually dull and dark in 19th-century imitation, by the impermanence of the decoration, by a certain lack of rapport between shape and decoration and by other subtle distinguishing features. Only a deep and first-hand knowledge of the originals can give the almost intuitive awareness of a forgery when all these negative factors leap to the eye in immediate proof.

The conclusion of this survey of European porcelain can legitimately be brief. By the first decades of the 19th century most of the famous factories had already closed, or else were on the point of closing, under the pressure of economic and political circumstances. For the factories which survived, and obviously these were the bigger ones, the 19th century produced nothing of great significance. Manufacturing processes became more and more mechanised, the best themes of the past were repeated through the use of old moulds, and little of original merit emerged.

From the first years of the present century, brave attempts were made to bring porcelain into line with the new currents of modern art. Art Nouveau suggested shapes and decorations to Meissen and to German factories in general during the early 1900s, while in more recent times pieces have often been influenced by the functional forms of industrial design. In Italy during the early 1940s notable modern pieces, inspired by classical art, were designed by Gio Ponti and Richard-Ginori. Sèvres made many valiant attempts to create modern shapes, and actually handled the paste in a new way in order to make the

29.   Sèvres. *Cache-pot. c.*1830. Musée des Arts Décoratifs, Paris. Typical product, with its heavy gilding, of the already exhausted phase of European porcelain. The subject belongs to the academic Romanticism which played such a large part in the literature and figurative arts of the 19th century.

30.   Paris. Plate. *c.*1860. Musée des Arts Décoratifs, Paris. Typical product of the bad taste of the late 19th century, weighed down by overcrowded decoration which combines many incongruous elements in the same way as this was being done in eclectic contemporary architecture.

31.   Paris. Figure of a lady. *c.*1880. Musée des Arts Décoratifs, Paris. Porcelain had by this time reached a high standard of virtuosity. Note for example the lace, which is done by dipping real lace in a semi-liquid solution of porcelain. Porcelain thus competed with contemporary painting and sculpture in its attention to detail.

32.   Paris. Figure of a woman. Polychrome biscuit. 1860. Musée des Arts Décoratifs, Paris. Like the previous statuette, this is an interesting illustration of contemporary fashion.

33.   Pouyat, Limoges. Tea-pot. *c.*1870. Musée des Arts Décoratifs, Paris. This, a product of late 19th-century industrialisation, looks for its inspiration to 18th-century shapes.

29

30. Paris. Plate. *c.*1860. Musée des Arts Décoratifs, Paris.

31. Paris. Figure of a lady. *c.*1880. Musée des arts Décoratifs, Paris.

32. Paris. Figure of a woman. Polychrome biscuit. 1860. Musée des Arts Décoratifs, Paris.

33. Pouyat, Limoges. Tea-pot. *c*.1870. Musée des Arts Décoratifs, Paris.

surfaces rough and uneven. This factory also invited famous artists, most notably Raoul Dufy, in its quest for new shapes and new decorative ideas, not only for special pieces but also for everyday table service. Even today, however, the old themes are wearily repeated time and again. Often shapes which derive from the 18th century are irrationally combined with Neo-classical decoration to satisfy a public taste which rejects what is new and unfamiliar in a medium whose essential character and potentialities, it seems, were fixed irrevocably during the century of its greatest glory.

MEISSEN FACTORY

The early years of the Meissen factory witnessed the discovery of European porcelain. The first pieces which Böttger presented to the King were teapots, cups, busts and reliefs in very hard red stoneware. The shapes were derived from contemporary silver-ware, with motifs in relief.

The discovery of kaolin however, the main source being Aue in Saxony, led to the use of white hard paste used chiefly for small pieces (little cups, goblets) with decorations in relief. By about 1720 the paste had already attained its almost definitive and perfect state. With Böttger dead in 1719, and the 'secret' already divulged in Vienna and Venice, the direction of the factory was, for about ten years, under Johann Hörold. Under his guidance the taste for *chinoiserie* ruled the day, and several of the German factory's most beautiful pieces date from this time. The shapes were almost exclusively derived from Eastern models as was the decoration, but although in the oriental style it was handled with more freedom and with European sensibility. A typical piece was a two-handled vase or amphora with a lid, either cylindrical or rectangular, slightly broadened at the rim, decorated with sprigs of leaves and flowers in vivid colours on a white ground.

About 1725 teapots, cups, jugs and bowls are decorated with little 'Chinese' scenes in colour or in gold, framed in a Rococo border in gold, brown and purplish-red. The 'oriental' scenes represent a fantastic world, created by the Western imagination on the lines of travellers' stories, missionaries' reports, and the oriental 'fables' which the European theatre loved to dramatise at that time. And as in Gozzi's *Turandot*, even tragic or cruel subjects are transformed into delicate fables. Other work typical of this first period are the unpainted pieces imported from the East and subsequently decorated at Meissen with the traditional themes of stylised oriental floral design. Pieces initialled by Hörold are very rare; we still have his designs but in most cases these would have been applied to the porcelain by journeyman decorators.

From the late 1730s the fashion for *chinoiserie* at the Meissen factory began to wane, even though the shapes still followed the traditional line. In place of pseudo-oriental scenes came 'European' scenes, inspired by genre painting and 17th-century Dutch landscapes, and portrayed with the same range of colours and the same liveliness as the oriental scenes. The oriental stylisation of flowers in the Chinese or

Korean manner gives place to the naturalness of 'Deutsche Blumen' (German flowers) arranged in bunches or on their own, with the apparent carelessness of Rococo decoration.

Porcelain statuettes began to be modelled at Meissen about 1730. At first there was even an attempt to compete with monumental sculpture in large-scale groups—there were plans, for example, for a huge equestrian statue of Augustus the Strong. But the difficulties involved in this kind of undertaking, in a material which, though resistant, was much less so than bronze or marble, led to the abandoning of the scheme. The first modeller under contract at Meissen (from 1727) was Johann Gottlieb Kirchner, who was responsible for a great many pieces, particularly animal figures. He was soon joined by Johann Joachim Kändler, who took over the direction of the works in 1733 and for over forty years was the leading figure at the Meissen works, his name being connected with the most important groups and figures produced there. There was no limit to the subject treated—satirical or merely farcical groups, scenes of gallantry, oriental figures and groups, animals, crafts and trades, religious and later mythological subjects, portraits of ruling princes, allegories (the arts, the seasons), and above all masked figures and scenes from the *commedia dell'arte*, captured in their most expressive and characteristic attitudes.

Under Kändler's direction also the Meissen works produced their most famous Baroque services, whose pieces—soup-tureens, coolers, sauce-boats—rivalled the porcelain statuettes in their plastic

34. Meissen. J. J. Kändler and Eberlein. Soup-tureen lid.
Kunstsammlung, Vienna.

35. Meissen. J. J. Kändler. *The Court Jesters Fröhlich and Schmiedel.* 1741. Porzellansammlung, Dresden.

36. Meissen. J. J. Kändler. *A Goat. c.*1732. Victoria and Albert Museum, London.

34.   Meissen. J. J. Kändler and Eberlein. Soup-tureen lid. Kunstsammlung, Vienna. This is a piece from the famous set known as the 'Swan service', done between 1737 and 1741 for the Count von Brühl.

35.   Meissen. J. J. Kändler. *The Court Jesters Fröhlich and Schmiedel.* 1741. Porzellansammlung, Dresden. One of the characteristics of Kändler's statuettes is their ironic and grotesque attitude, more or less pronounced, which in this case is perfectly suited to the artist's chosen subject.

36.   Meissen. J. J. Kändler. *A Goat.* c.1732. Victoria and Albert Museum, London. Animal subjects were among the favourites of Kändler and the Saxon factory in general, especially in its early years. Notice the animal's natural position, and the close observation reflecting the scientific interest in the animal world which developed during the 18th century.

37.   Meissen. J. J. Kändler. Figure of a woman. Kunstgewer-bemuseum, Hamburg. The gestures and lightly caricatured attitudes of his figures are a perfect reflection, in an ironic key, of the affectation of social life at that time.

designs. Examples are the Sulkowsky service, made for a famous Imperial Marshal of that name, to a design dominated by the figures of lions rampant, bearing his coat-of-arms; the Swan service, made for the Count von Bruhl, with the huge white birds as its main decorative theme; and in 1738 a service, decorated with landscapes and scenes *à la Watteau* in green monochrome for Maria Amalia of Saxony, for her marriage to the King of Naples. The 'everyday' services of this time have a white base with decorations in relief, in the form of sprigs and basketwork, along the edges, and are painted with *Deutsche Blumen* in many colours. In such cases, too, there is modelling in the knobs on the lids (where 'putti' or female figures act as knobs), or in handles which are designed as complicated floral compositions.

Between 1740 and 1750 Meissen was also at a commercial as well as an aesthetic peak. It exported to the Ottoman Empire, and indulged in exotic themes which were in doubtful taste to European eyes, but sure of their effect on the Eastern market. It exported to Russia, where a porcelain factory, later to be supported by Catherine the Great, had just been founded. Meissen also exported to England, and even to France, where a daughter of Augustus II had married the Dauphin. But the years of the factory's ascendancy ended with the Seven Years War (1756– 1763). Frederick II of Prussia, after his victories in Saxony, wanted to move the whole Meissen works to Berlin at once, and did succeed in taking over the greater part of it, which passed into the Berlin factory when this was acquired by the Prussian government.

In 1761, after peace had been declared, the Saxon works started production again, but was now dominated by Sèvres in matters of both form and design. During the first forty years of European porcelain, Meissen had been the law-giver; after 1760 the Sèvres taste enjoyed an almost absolute authority. Kändler died in 1775; his last task was the great service for Catherine of Russia. His death marks the end of the great days of Saxon porcelain.

From 1774 to 1814 the factory was under the direction of Camillo Marcolini. It was a time of complicated developments—at first academic themes which re-echo more coldly the *Deutsche Blumen* and the traditional shapes, then the Biedermeier period, when the prevailing taste was for heavy gildings, violent contrasts and clashes of colour.

Marks. The first pieces in stoneware produced by Böttger were stamped with two small crossed swords. The first hard porcelain has as its mark the King's monogram, 'AR', intertwined, or else the initials of the works—'KPM' or 'KPF', Königliche Porzellan-Manufaktur or Fabrik, that is, Royal Porcelain Works or Factory. Less common marks are a kind of kite, and the caduceus, which is a spiral winding round a vertical line. But already in its first period we find the sign which was to be, and still is, typical of Meissen, namely, the two crossed swords, sometimes stamped into the porcelain but more often painted in blue.

After about 1730 a dot is sometimes added, either under or between the swords, while in Marcolini's time there is always an asterisk under the two swords.

38. Meissen. Salver with oriental decorations. *c*.1735.
Victoria and Albert Museum, London.

VIENNA FACTORY

As has been seen in the introduction, the second hard porcelain factory to open after Meissen was that at Vienna founded by Innocentius du Paquier with the assistance of Hunger and Stölzel, two deserters from Meissen. Du Paquier himself was a senior functionary in the Imperial household and was granted, by the Emperor Charles VI, a twenty-five year 'privilege' for the manufacture of porcelain within Imperial Austrian territory. The kaolin for the factory, which came from the Passau quarries, gave the ware a vaguely milky colour; the first years' production was not very high, and above all the process was very costly. All sorts of devices were tried, such as lotteries, for example, but none succeeded in selling the product which was as yet not in great public demand. To make matters worse, the two arcanists from Meissen were discontented, and left Vienna. In 1744 the works became state property.

The early output of the Viennese factory included an enormous variety of shapes and decorative themes. Forms which were vaguely Eastern alternated with pieces still influenced by the late Baroque taste, which was mainly derived from the work of contemporary gold- and silversmiths. In the 1730s Eastern or 'Indian' decorative themes, as they were incorrectly called, appeared side by side with *Deutsche Blumen*, sometimes in a more naturalistic mood than those from the Saxon factory, or with the so-called *Laub-und Bandwerk* (literally 'garland ribbon designs'), typical of the Austrian factory. A kind of *horror vacui*

38. Meissen. Salver with oriental decorations. *c*.1735. Victoria and Albert Museum, London. The moulded form of the salver is typically European, derived from contemporary silverware. The decoration, however, reflects, though more nimbly, the traditional themes of oriental decoration, from the shape of the foliage to the elegant outline of the bird, both inspired by imported articles.

39. Vienna. J. Niedermeyer. Salt. *c*.1750. Victoria and Albert Museum, London. Important services included some pieces, like this salt, which were designed as groups but which also had a function as decorative tableware. Johann Joseph Niedermeyer, the leading modeller known to us at the Viennese factory, came from the Vienna Academy. In 1747 he was appointed chief modeller at the porcelain factory.

40. Vienna. Soup-tureen with lid bearing Imperial Russian coat-of-arms. 1735–1744. Victoria and Albert Museum, London. All the factory's decorative characteristics are concentrated in this fine piece from du Paquier's Vienna works—masks and stylised trimmings, interlaced patterns and flowers in relief, on a shape which is faithfully copied from contemporary silverware. The service was a gift from Charles VI to the Tsar of Russia.

40. Vienna. Soup-tureen with lid bearing Imperial Russian coat-of-arms. 1735–1744. Victoria and Albert Museum, London.

seemed to dominate the decorators of this first phase, especially after about 1730; the surfaces of the pieces are not only decorated with ornaments in relief or with figurative medallions, but are often almost entirely covered in interwoven geometrical patterns on wreath and trellis themes. Purple and yellow, red and green, blue and gold are the predominant colours of the Viennese factory's first period. In 1744 du Paquier gave up the works, being bought out by the Empress Maria Theresa. But the factory was again near to disaster when in about 1780 it tried to imitate the Rococo decorations of Sèvres—by that time the arbiter of taste in European porcelain. The Viennese works in fact tried to imitate the purity and lightness of the French factory's porcelain, without taking into account the fact that Sèvres soft past was made from altogether different components and had quite different potentialities. And although the painter Schindler excelled in decorations *à la Watteau*, and the factory's chief modeller, the sculptor Niedermayer, was outstanding in figure-groups still largely derived from Meissen, Vienna ware never approached, either in shape or in decoration, the lightness of the French pieces.

Meanwhile in 1778 Antonio Grassi, a young man of Italian origin, who had been a pupil of Messerschmidt, was taken on as assistant to Niedermayer. He began by favouring the familiar themes—Arcadian or 'bourgeois' groups—but a long trip to Italy, with visits to Florence, Rome and Naples, was decisive in turning him towards the Neo-classicism which was to influence the Austrian factory's sculpture.

After 1784, under the direction of Konrad von Sorgenthal, the Vienna works achieved a financial stability for the first time. But the great century of porcelain was now drawing to its close. Typical Neo-classical pieces from the Viennese factory were the many services whose cups, pots and vases were rigidly cylindrical in shape, decorated lavishly with generous use of gold, shining, matt or in low relief. Often all three gilding treatments were combined to form decorative borders and fillets whose designs, handled in the 18th-century naturalistic tradition, became increasingly stylised until they resolved themselves in purely geometrical strokes. New colours, many of which were the result of the researches of the chemist Joseph Leithner, were introduced, some of them extremely artificial—sharp lemon yellow, salmon pink, cyclamen, violet, grey and various very intense blues.

Under the guidance of Grassi Vienna achieved an enormous output, in the field of sculpture, almost exclusively in biscuit ware. Arcadian views and amorous scenes, figures from the Italian Comedy, scenes of domestic life which had been rediscovered by the 'intimism' of the late 18th century, were succeeded by classical groups, and the Olympian deities, often inspired by the great classical sculpture which Neo-classicism venerated. As well as these there were portraits of princes, with a complicated accompaniment of allegorical accessories, aimed at exalting the virtues of contemporary rulers.

After Sorgenthal's death in 1805, the factory carried on under Matthias Niedermayer, in spite of the upheavals of the wars which convulsed Europe in those years. After 1810, the Vienna works tolerated the heavy Biedermeier taste which left its mark on everything, from fashions to furniture, from architecture to painting, and it had ceased to contribute anything of originality for some years before it finally closed in 1864.

Marks. Pieces dating from du Paquier's time are not marked. After 1744, when the factory was taken over by the state, a shield divided by a horizontal band was introduced as a mark, and this was first stamped on the porcelain and later painted in blue. After 1784, for example, pieces are stamped with the serial number and the year '97' for 1797 or '802' for 1802.

LESSER GERMAN FACTORIES

In the space of twelve years, starting in 1746, there was a great increase of hard porcelain factories on German territory. They took their shapes and decorative themes from the leading factories of Meissen, and, later, Sèvres.

Höchst. Founded in 1746, under the patronage of the Archbishop Elector of Mainz, was best known for the figures modelled by J. P. Melchior, who worked there from 1767 to 1779. Inspired by the usual subjects, they can be recognised by their delicate modelling and their soft and, as it were, rounded shapes. The mark is a wheel, the heraldic sign of Mainz, stamped in the porcelain or painted in various colours.

Berlin. Founded in 1749 by Wegely, a private citizen, from 1751 onwards it had Frederick of Prussia as its patron. The raw material came from the quarry at Aue in Saxony. In 1761 the factory was taken over by Gotzkowsky at a particularly difficult moment, at the climax of the Seven Years War. The Prussian King's victory decided the fate of the factory, which became state property in 1763 when, as has been mentioned, Frederick the Great at once attempted to dismantle Meissen and transfer it to Berlin. Typical products of the Berlin factory are pieces decorated in relief and painted in particularly brilliant colours (pink and green predominating). The paste is exceptionally bright and fine.

Marks. 'W' in the Wegely period, 'G' in that of Gotzkowsky. A blue sceptre when the works were taken over by the state. During the 19th century the initials 'KFM' surmounted by a crown.

Fürstenberg. The Fürstenberg porcelain factory, founded by Carl I in 1747, is the oldest in the German Federal Republic. From 1753 the blue 'F', later surmounted by a crown, was used as a mark of manufacture and of quality by the factory whose wares achieved a notable artistic level while at the same time imitating Meissen forms and motifs in dishes and figurines. In the years 1754–1755 Simon Feilner designed the famous group of figures from the *commedia dell'arte* which was sold at auction in London in 1960 for £15,000. The Fürstenberg factory produced an enormous output of Neo-classical wares, which came to an end in the first decades of the 19th

41. Berlin. F. E. Meyer. *Shepherd.* Kunstgewerbemuseum, Cologne.

41.   Berlin. F. E. Meyer. *Shepherd*. Kunstgewerbemuseum, Cologne. The pastoral theme, more or less sophisticated, is one of the favourite subjects of porcelain modelling in the 18th century. Friedrich Elias Meyer worked in the Berlin factory from 1761, having left Meissen during the Seven Years War.

42.   Nymphenburg. F. A. Bustelli. *Julia*. *c*.1760. Bayerisches Nationalmuseum, Munich. This is another of the sixteen famous figures of characters from the *commedia dell'arte,* modelled shortly before his death by Bustelli. It is perhaps one of the best known, because of the grace of the pose.

43.   Ludwigsburg. J. C. W. Beyer. *The Cup of Coffee*. *c*.1765. Kunstgewerbemuseum, Hamburg. Coffee, together with chocolate, was one of the popular new drinks of the 18th century. And so figures like this can be seen in European porcelain, as in the pictures of Longhi and Fragonard.

44.   Nymphenburg. F. A. Bustelli. *Anselm*. Kunstgewerbemuseum, Hamburg. This is another character from the *commedia dell'arte* series. They were modelled in pairs with corresponding colour schemes and gestures. The figure of Anselm is paired with that of Corinna.

42

43. Ludwigsburg. J. C. W. Beyer. *The Cup of Coffee.* c.1765. Kunstgewerbemuseum, Hamburg.

44. Nymphenburg. F. A. Bustelli. *Anselm*. Kunstgewerbemuseum, Hamburg.

century when designs were adapted to conform with the changing taste of the times. Wares are at present being produced in Baroque and Empire styles, but the factory has also made some successful modern designs.

Nymphenburg. The factory, whose first efforts go back to about 1747, owed its success to the patronage of Maximilian III, Duke of Bavaria, and to the intelligent direction of Sigismund von Heimhausen, whose portrait-bust in porcelain by Bustelli is one of the finest portraits of 18th-century Europe. Like all the other south German factories, it got its raw material from the Passau quarries. The crowning glory of the Nymphenburg factory is Francesco Antonio Bustelli, from the Ticino, one of the greatest sculptors of 18th-century Europe. As well as the famous sixteen figures from the *commedia dell'arte*, Bustelli, who was at the height of his powers in about 1760, also modelled oriental figures and scenes, and Arcadian and pastoral subjects. He had an exceptionally ironic and disillusioned vein, which expressed itself in elegant contortions, desperate leaps, attitudes which were exaggerated without ever becoming grotesque or vulgar. He brought out the whole mood and personality of his characters, who always seem to be on the point of bursting into the cavatina of a comic opera.

The Nymphenburg mark is the Bavarian shield, criss-crossed and stamped in the porcelain, while Bustelli's pieces are often marked with their maker's initials.

Frankenthal. The early history of the Frankenthal

factory was unusual. In 1752 Paul Hannong, a member of a family with a long connection with ceramics, opened a hard paste porcelain factory at Strasbourg, which was at that time in French territory. But he was soon obliged to move his works across the frontier into Germany, because Sèvres obstructed in every possible way the first French hard porcelain factory which could be a serious threat to its own monopoly.

The works were transferred to Frankenthal in the Palatinate, and in 1755 the Elector Carl Theodor first offered them a 'privilege'; seven years later the factory became directly dependent on him.

As well as the usual products, vases and dishes which were once again modelled on Meissen, Frankenthal produced a great many groups and statuettes, the most important of the many chief modellers at the factory being Friedrich Lück, Konrad Link and J. P. Melchior, who was working at Höchst before he came to Frankenthal. As elsewhere in Europe so at Frankenthal, the influence of Sèvres superseded that of Meissen in the second half of the century.

The factory's marks are very varied. The early products have a lion rampant, in blue, with Hannong's initials. Later work bears a monogram made up of the interwoven initials of the Elector, in various forms, surmounted by a crown.

Ludwigsburg. Founded in 1758 by Duke Carl Eugen of Württemberg as 'indispensable to the pomp and dignity' of the throne, Ludwigsburg had a comparatively short life-span. It produced a limited range of ware—which was all decorated with

45. Höchst. *Dancer with Cymbals*. 1775. Victoria and
Albert Museum, London.

great flamboyance and with generous use of modelling in relief.

Its groups and figures were of a very high quality although the factory did not, in fact, have any very resounding names among its modellers. The porcelain, using kaolin from the Passau quarries, is slightly greyish.

The mark was formed from the Duke's initials, interwoven in various ways, sometimes surmounted by a crown.

These factories, together with Meissen, were seven leading German works. Of the many lesser ones, the most important is the Fulda factory founded by the Prince Bishop Heinrich von Bibra in 1765, but closed as early as 1780. It is famous for the excellence of its groups and figures, which are now very rare and sought-after today. The mark is a dark blue cross, or two cursive 'F's (*Fürstliche Fulda*) intertwined and surmounted by a cross.

VEZZI (VENICE)

The Vezzi works at Venice was the first Italian porcelain factory. It had a very short life because of the precarious ups-and-downs of the early European factories and its lack of wealthy 'protectors'.

Francesco Vezzi was a goldsmith who was passionately interested in ceramic research. In 1720 he was joined by Hunger, the restless emigrant from Meissen after he moved on from Vienna. Theirs was indeed the earliest and for a long time the only hard paste factory in Italy, the kaolin they used being smuggled over the border from the Aue mines in Saxony.

The few pieces surviving from this first Venetian factory are sometimes confused with those from Vienna during du Paquier's time. Shapes range between oriental and late Baroque, decorations are in relief, flowers, animals, large masks and grotesque subjects, in the manner already elaborated by Hunger in Vienna; it must be remembered that both Hunger and Vezzi had excelled as goldsmiths, and brought to the new material the taste for surfaces worked in relief, and *repoussé* typical of contemporary goldsmiths' work.

The Italian factory also produced teapots, cups, vases and *chinoiserie,* painted in vivid colours—deep reds, greens, yellows, blues. But the faithless Hunger left Venice too, returned to Meissen and, perhaps to obtain forgiveness for his double betrayal, divulged that the secret material, the kaolin from Aue, was being clandestinely exported to Venice. From that moment supplies of Saxon kaolin were cut off from the Italian factory, which tried instead to use the white clay of the Tretto, near Vicenza. But this contained a low percentage of kaolin, and the results were unsatisfactory; the grey paste was less plastic and experiments to improve it were costly. In 1727 the unhappy career of the first Italian porcelain factory was over.

The mark of the Vezzi factory is the word 'Venice', either written in full or else abbreviated to 'Ven'.

DOCCIA

In 1735 a Tuscan nobleman, the Marchese Carlo Ginori, who took an interest in chemical research, set up a porcelain factory near Florence. On a visit to Vienna, with a delegation of Tuscan aristocrats, to pay their respects to the new Grand Duke (of Habsburg-Lorraine), who had been elected to succeed the last of the Medici line, Ginori made the acquaintance of Karl Anreiter, painter and decorator at the Vienna works, and Giorgio delle Torri, a very able technologist, and persuaded them to follow him to Florence. The first trials at the Doccia factory, made with Tuscan clay, had yielded very poor results, as the defective grey paste cracked and warped during the firing. With the help of the two Viennese 'arcanists', however, satisfactory results were eventually obtained about the year 1740 and Ginori gained a twenty-year 'privilege' from Francesco of Lorraine, the new Grand Duke of Tuscany. The paste was composed of clays from the island of Elba, with quartz from Seravezza and the white clays of the Tretto. Among the first local workers, who were ready to replace the two Viennese when they left Doccia a few years later, were the 'chemist' Jacopo Fanciullacci and the modeller Gaspero Bruschi, who were to be succeeded at the Tuscan factory by generations of fine craftsmen.

The first marketable products were plates and jars decorated in stencil in blue, with lightly stylised floral designs, and a series of pieces, mostly cups and trays, decorated by Anreiter with landscapes, costumed figures, and still-life taken from paintings or

46. Doccia. Coffee-pot with coat-of-arms of Cardinal
Stoppani. *c.*1775. Victoria and Albert Museum, London.

drawings of the Tuscan school. A difficult and rare achievement of these early years were the so-called double-walled vases, with openwork outer surfaces. After Carlo Ginori died, the direction of the factory passed to his eldest son Lorenzo though not without violent and continuing clashes between him and his brothers. Under Lorenzo's leadership, however (1757–91), the factory made great strides, and the period saw the creation of its most famous pieces and services, which derived their shapes and decoration mainly from oriental designs or from German ware, such as the pieces with flowers, animals and sprigs in relief. There are services described in the factory brochure as made 'in the Chinese manner' and under this name is perhaps included the best known, now called the 'tulipano', where the central element of the stylised floral decoration is a red flower with ragged-edged petals. Others were described as 'Saxon style' (framed scenes like those of Meissen), 'with figured bas-reliefs', with landscapes painted in purple-red or different colours, with flowers 'in bunches', some, especially at the end of the 18th century, in rustic mood.

After the first attempts at large-scale modelling of porcelain statues, Doccia fell back on small-scale figures. The chief modeller, Gaspero Bruschi, and his grandson Giuseppe were responsible for most of the Doccia statuettes, allegorical figures of the seasons and the arts, shepherds and putti. Designs for other pieces, however, above all scenes from mythology or sacred groups, were derived from 17th-century and also contemporary Florentine sculpture.

The term *'masso bastardo'* which, from their grey and uneven paste, is commonly applied to the oldest pieces, does not occur in the factory's papers before 1765, and it indicates an inferior type of paste, mainly obtained with clays from Montecarlo near Lucca, and covered with a thick tin glaze.

The Doccia factory was also affected by the Neo-classical taste at the end of the 18th century, and this is reflected in stiffer shapes and more formal decoration.

About 1810, under the guidance of the young Carlo Leopoldo, the shapes and decoration of Doccia ware came into line with the heavy taste which prevailed at that time, and which revelled in gold, in bulky forms, the so-called *'sbavata'* cup which was widened towards the top, and in heavy decorations in relief. In 1821 Doccia acquired the models from the Naples factory which were being scattered or destroyed, and statuettes and dishes from the Naples works were repeated at Doccia in hard paste, and were initialled with the letter 'N' which is the distinguishing mark of the Naples factory. The Doccia factory also specialised in the making of replacements for broken pieces of important services from other works. Many pieces from the Grand Duke's services, which can still be seen at the Museo degli Argenti at the Pitti Palace, were replaced by the Doccia factory. They were almost always marked with the factory's star, and are seldom as fine as the lost originals, either in composition or in decoration. The factory remained in the possession of the Ginori family till 1896, when it merged with the ceramic company Richard of Milan.

The mark of Doccia, whose early pieces are often signed but not initialled by their decorators, makes a rather late appearance, and is a star (in the form of an asterisk) in red or gold, to be found on the better pieces. Later, in the 19th century, the star was replaced by the name of the factory, written in full.

CAPODIMONTE, BUEN RETIRO, NAPLES

These three factories are best dealt with in one section since they were all three closely connected with the history of the ruling house of Bourbon in Spain and Naples during the 18th century.

Capodimonte. In 1738 Maria Amalia, daughter of Augustus III of Saxony and grand-daughter of Augustus the Strong, married Charles VII, King of the Two Sicilies. She brought as part of her dowry a great deal of porcelain and a famous green and gold service, painted with scenes *à la Watteau* at the family works. Charles VII, wanting to emulate his father-in-law and to comply with his wife's wishes, founded a porcelain factory at Capodimonte in 1743, but the search for a source of kaolin within the king's domains proved fruitless. The Capodimonte porcelain is, in consequence, a soft paste, and was developed by the two 'chemists', Livio and Gaetano Schepers, who got their raw material from Calabrian clays.

Capodimonte's fame is mainly connected with its celebrated statuettes and with the Porcelain Room at Portici (Plate 51), later moved to the palace at Capodimonte. These famous pieces steal the limelight from

45. Höchst. *Dancer with cymbals*. 1775. Victoria and Albert Museum, London. Exotic figures were among the favourite subjects of European porcelain; oriental things played a great part in the figurative art of the 18th century. The curved rhythm of this figure is very elegant, and is probably the work of J. P. Melchior, who was model master at Höchst from 1767 to 1779.

46. Doccia. Coffee-pot with coat-of-arms of Cardinal Stoppani. *c*.1775. Victoria and Albert Museum, London. This is a typical shape from the Tuscan factory towards the middle of the century. It was customary for noble and royal families, and for high dignitaries of Church and state, to have their personal services decorated with their family coats-of-arms and crests.

47. Naples. *Family Group*. *c*.1780. Museo di Capodimonte, Naples. After the Naples factory reopened in 1771, the subjects of statuettes also changed in conformity with the taste of the time. On the one hand there were historical or mythological themes to satisfy the new Neo-classical fashion; on the other there were scenes of domestic intimacy, as in this picture of everyday life, of which there were many different versions. The chief modeller at Capodimonte during this period was Camillo Celebrano.

47

the fine services with their floral, mythological or exotic decoration, and from the 'knick-knacks' such as snuffboxes, which the factory also produced. In the mid 1740s the chief modeller at the factory, and later director of the works until 1759, was Giuseppe Gricc, son-in-law of Livio Schepers. The favourite subject of the Capodimonte statuettes and groups was above all the figures of the *commedia dell'arte*, in which the buffooneries of the Italian comedy are captured and fixed in realistic and lively attitudes. Another genre at the Neapolitan works was popular types and characters, sometimes deliberately carica- tured, or scenes taken from ancient mythology (successfully repeated at a later date by the Buen Retiro factory) in which the heroes are of the same stamp as the languid actors in Metastasio's plays.

The Portici Porcelain Room was done between 1757 and 1759, and is one of the most remarkable products of this aspect of the 18th-century European passion for porcelain. It is a small room, whose walls are covered with slabs of porcelain, decorated in relief with oriental figures and with sprigs and vegeta- tion which stand out in vivid colours against the white background. A chandelier and candlesticks, also in porcelain, complete the room.

There has been, and still is, an enormous amount of faking of Capodimonte ware. The earliest imitations go back to the mid 19th century. Fakes can, however, be easily recognised by those who have some acquaint- ance with the originals. They sometimes give them- selves away by the excessive weight of the paste, by their rough and careless modelling—whereas the surfaces of original pieces, though often treated swiftly and artificially, remained fluid and exact—by their heavy and gaudy gilding which is duller in comparison with the lustre of 18th-century gold, and by their violent and disagreeable clashes of colour. It should also be noted that pieces from the new Neapolitan factory, which reopened in 1771, often pass as Capodimonte, while another source of confusion was the fact that after the move to Buen Retiro in Spain, described below, some of the few artisans who were left behind at Naples took the opportunity of faking work and marketing pieces on their own account under the name of Capodimonte.

The Capodimonte mark consists of the Bourbon lily, stylised in violet or blue.

Buen Retiro. On the death of his brother Ferdinand VI, King Charles of the Two Sicilies acceded to the Spanish throne in 1759 with the title Charles III. He thereupon transferred the Capodimonte factory, machines, moulds and workmen, to Buen Retiro near Madrid. Gaetano Schepers and Giuseppe Gricc remained in charge of the works, to be succeeded by their sons or brothers. One of the earliest undertakings of the new factory was a replica of the Portici Porcelain Room in the Palace of Aranjuez (1760–1763), and afterwards the creation of another, in a colder and more academic mood, in the royal palace at Madrid (1765–1770).

Often identical in shape and decoration with the Capodimonte pieces, the products of the Spanish factory's first period can be distinguished from the Italian ware by the different quality of the paste, obtained with clay from the Vallecas quarry, which has an oily appearance and a greenish tone. After about 1770 historical or mythological groups and figures take the place of the scenes from everyday life or the *commedia dell'arte*, while after 1780 the Spanish factory, which had meanwhile tried to improve its paste by adding a feldspathic clay which gave it greater resistance, took its subjects from the first Neo-classical pieces from the factories of Sèvres, the Duke of Angoulême, and Wedgwood. Excellent copies in biscuit of classical statues and busts date from the late 18th century.

The death of Charles III in 1788 marks the end of the factory's best period; in the same year sales were opened to the public, but the enterprise was a failure because the prices were too high. The factory, a king's costly caprice, continued to work almost exclusively to supply the needs of the court. Dismantled by French troops in 1808, during the Napoleonic wars, the works were completely sacked and destroyed by the people in 1818, when the troops of the restored Spanish house withdrew. The factory of La Moncloa, which opened shortly afterwards, was of little importance.

The mark of Buen Retiro is the same as that of Capodimonte.

Portici, Naples. One of the first acts of King Ferdinand IV of Naples, when he was scarcely of age—he was only just eighteen when he was elected king—was to open a new porcelain factory at Portici in 1771. Two years later the works was transferred to Naples, specialists being recruited from among the few old

48. Naples. Painted by Antonio Zuccarelli. Vase with portrait of Murat. Museo Napoleonico, Rome.

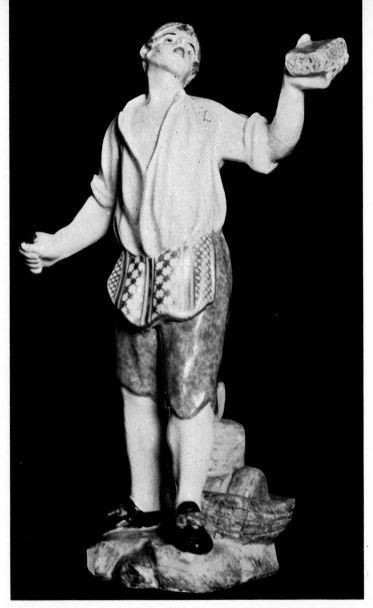

49. Capodimonte. *The Cakeseller*. Museo di Capodimonte, Naples.

50. Capodimonte. *The Vendor of Plaster Busts*. Museo di Capodimonte, Naples.

48.   Naples. Painted by Antonio Zuccarelli. Vase with portrait of Murat. Museo Napoleonico, Rome. The Naples factory followed the fashion set by Sèvres in dedicating many vases and complete services to the glories of Napoleon. These pieces were decorated with a whole array of symbols, emblems, classical shapes and above all a quantity of lavish gold, which underlined their regal character.

49.   Capodimonte. *The Cakeseller*. Museo di Capodimonte, Naples. Trades were among the favourite subjects of porcelain sculpture, and these were chosen from the most picturesque and colourful callings. This piece, like the next one, was done while the chief modeller at the Capodimonte factory was Giuseppe Gricc (1743–1759).

50.   Capodimonte. *The Vendor of Plaster Busts*. Museo di Capodimonte, Naples. This belongs to the same series as the previous piece and, like it, dates from about 1750 to 1755. The modelling of the Capodimonte statuettes is flowing and swift; gestures and attitudes are captured with a happy and quick intuition.

51.   Capodimonte. Porcelain Room. Museo di Capodimonte, Naples. This is the most remarkable product of the Capodimonte factory. The Porcelain Room, made between 1757 and 1759 for the palace at Portici, and later moved to Capodimonte, was done for Maria Amalia of Saxony, the King's mother. It consists of a small room which is entirely walled in slabs of white porcelain, with *chinoiserie* coloured in relief.   51

workers from the Capodimonte factory who had not emigrated to Madrid in 1759.

The opening of the Naples factory coincided with the great Neo-classical movement in Europe, and Naples, with the discoveries at Herculaneum and Pompeii, was one of the centres of this revival. Vases imitated classical shapes, amphorae, hydriae, kraters, while whole services were modelled in the Greek or Etruscan styles and, after the Napoleonic campaign in Egypt, in the Egyptian style as well. Statuary drew abundantly on antique sculpture, translating its great works into the diminutive dimensions of biscuit porcelain. The great classical pieces from the Farnese collection at Naples offered modellers at the factory an endless supply of examples and inspiration: *The Punishment of Dirce, The Judgment of Paris, Chiron and Achilles, The Rape of Europa* are the titles of some of the most famous groups modelled by Camillo Celebrano. Decoration too was dominated by mythological subjects, views of the recent excavations, or neat exact landscapes in the style of Vanvitelli.

The search had continued for new compounds and in 1772 the first hard paste was produced, which was later improved upon. But in 1798, on the approach of French troops, Ferdinand fled to Sicily, and the factory was sacked. It reopened a year later, but effectively came to an end with Ferdinand's second flight in 1806 and, as we have seen, the models belonging to the Neapolitan factory were purchased by C. L. Ginori at Capodimonte.

The mark of Naples ware is 'N' or the King's initials, surmounted by a crown.

LESSER ITALIAN FACTORIES

Within the bounds of the Venetian Republic, where the ceramic industry had a strong tradition, numerous maiolica works attempted, during the second half of the 18th century, to repeat the venture in which Vezzi had failed.

Le Nove. In 1752 the Antonibon family from Le Nove di Bassano began to produce the first 'samples' of porcelain. These were later presented to the Venetian Republic, which granted the factory exemptions and privileges. The best period of these works, which produced mainly tableware with landscapes and pastoral scenes, was between 1760 and 1780. But the factory was always beset by difficulties, and from the mid 1760s was further crippled by the continual resignations of the best workmen. They either left the factory to work on their own account, as in the case of the d'Este factory, which opened with a staff of deserters from Le Nove, or else they accepted the tempting offers of Geminiano Cozzi, who had opened a factory in Venice.

The porcelain from the Antonibons' factory is opaque and rather grey; the mark, a six-pointed star in the form of an asterisk in red or gold, is often accompanied by the name of the factory, written in full.

Cozzi. The factory which Geminiano Cozzi, a banker from Modena, opened in the S. Giobbe district of Venice in 1764 enjoyed remarkable success for a time. Launched in the second half of the century, when the experimental period of European porcelain was already at an end, it was able to take advantage of technical progress already acquired, without having to pour capital investment into trials and experiments. But it closed in 1812, when it too was overwhelmed by the profound changes in European taste, patronage and political structure which brought about the downfall of the world which had given birth to and fostered the great age of porcelain in Europe.

Cozzi's factory was greatly helped by orders from the many coffee-houses which played such an important part in 18th-century Venetian life. Cups and coffee-jugs from the factory, which was moreover the exclusive retailer to the houses of Venetian nobles and wealthy citizens, can be recognised in Longhi's genre paintings, or scenes from everyday life. It also appears that Cozzi provided the government of the Venetian Republic, free of charge, with all the dishes needed for state ceremonies and receptions. In exchange for this he was granted enormous favours—protective customs, restrictions on all foreign porcelain, exemption from heavy taxes, and other privileges of various kinds. Success was almost inevitable for a firm holding such a monopolistic position.

A great deal of the decoration of the factory's products was derived from the figurative tradition of 18th-century Venice, and the services which were decorated with landscapes drawn from the paintings of Zais and Zuccarelli were particularly successful.

The raw material came from the Tretto quarry near Vicenza, which had already been used by Vezzi and

52. Le Nove di Bassano. *Venus appearing before Aeneas.*
*c.*1785. Ca' Rezzonico, Venice.

53

52.   Le Nove di Bassano. *Venus appearing before Aeneas*. *c*.1785. Ca' Rezzonico, Venice. The subject is classical, but the mood is still that of Metastasio's languid heroes. The factory of Le Nove grew out of an old maiolica factory, adapted towards the mid 1700s to produce articles in porcelain.

53.   Vinovo. *Diana*. After a bronze by the 16th-century sculptor Giambologna in the Bargello, Florence. End of the 18th century. Victoria and Albert Museum, London. It became a common practice, from the late 18th century till well on in the 19th, to render the great classical statues in the small dimensions of porcelain, and above all in biscuit. It is rarer to find such reproductions of 16th-century statues.

54.   Le Nove di Bassano. Tea-pot. *c*.1765. Victoria and Albert Museum, London. The shape is derived from contemporary silverware. Note the decoration in relief, which corresponds to *repoussé* metalwork. The landscape is inspired by the Venetian Arcadian landscapes of the 18th century by Zais and Zuccarelli.

55.   Cozzi, Venice. Coffee-pot. *c*.1770. Victoria and Albert Museum, London. This is a very common shape from the Venetian factory, which was the main supplier in the second half of the 18th century to the Venetian Republic, to the noble households and to the many coffee-houses in the city.

54. Le Nove di Bassano. Tea-pot. *c.*1765. Victoria and Albert Museum, London.

55. Cozzi, Venice. Coffee-pot. *c.*1770. Victoria and Albert Museum, London.

the Doccia works (in their early years at least). The paste, considered 'hard' or 'hybrid', has a slightly grey tone, like all paste made from clays found near the Tretto.

The mark of the Cozzi factory is an anchor, usually in red, but often also in blue and in gold.

Vinovo. The Vinovo works, founded in 1775 under the patronage of the King of Piedmont, had a royal privilege for the manufacture of soft paste. After a period of critically bad administration it was reopened in 1780 by the chemist Vittorio Amedeo Gioannetti; it finally closed in 1824. The paste developed by Gioannetti is considered hard, and is ivory-coloured with a large admixture of quartz and magnesite. The factory produced services and small statues, in which Saxon designs merge with French ones. Vinovo's mark is a 'V', surmounted by a small cross, later accompanied by the letters 'DG' (Doctor Gioannetti) in blue.

Volpato. At Rome, from 1785 to 1831 the Volpato factory worked to produce an exclusively Neo-classical output, mainly in biscuit, which reproduced the great classical statues on a small scale. Another famous series from the Volpato works is the one of costumes of the Roman *campagna,* all modelled in biscuit. The mark is the name of the factory, in full, stamped on the paste.

VINCENNES FACTORY (SÈVRES)

In 1738 Louis XV granted the brother of his Finance Minister, Orry de Fulvy, a 'privilege' for the establishment of a porcelain factory in the 'Saxon style', though for the next thirty years it was concerned exclusively with soft paste. Two brothers, Gilles and Robert Dubois, who had left Chantilly, probably dismissed because of bad conduct, worked in the new factory, which was at first housed in the Château de Vincennes. In such circumstances it is hardly surprising that the earliest attempts were unsuccessful; the Vincennes factory, which was to inherit the tradition and the achievements of the greatest German works, finally owed its success to François Gravant and to Jean Hellot, a 'chemist' from the Parisian Académie des Sciences. In 1753 the factory was taken under royal protection at the instigation of Madame de Pompadour, the King's mistress, with the title 'Manufacture Royale des Porcelaines de France'. In 1756 the factory was moved to Sèvres and four years later became the property of the King outright. In 1768 after kaolin had been discovered in the neighbourhood of St Yrieix la Perche, it began to produce its first hard paste, although for years it also continued its former tradition of soft paste.

From its earliest years Vincennes-Sèvres ware was outstanding for beauty of shape and decoration; vases, jars, amphorae, *cache pots* and services have a flowing and most elegant design, with handles forming sprigs and flowering branches, knobs representing flowers or buds, and spouts made out of coils of thin leaves.

From the first, the capacity of soft paste for taking a wide range of rich colours was exploited to the full—turquoise, the deep 'royal blue', the extraordinary

56

56. Vincennes. Blondeau. *The Young Suppliant*. 1752. Sèvres Museum. Blondeau was a modeller at Vincennes, and his masterpiece is the series of eight figures of children, of which this is one, taken from models by Boucher. In French porcelain sculpture, alongside the piquant and amorous scenes, there is a whole range of sentimental ones. These were increasingly popular at the end of the 18th century and are well represented by this appealing figure in biscuit, intended to be delicately *larmoyant*.

57. Sèvres. Decorated by Evans. Cup and saucer. 1762. Musée des Arts Décoratifs, Paris. Etienne Evans was a specialist in bird and animal paintings; another piece by him is reproduced in Plate 16. Birds, together with flowers, were among the favourite decorative subjects at Sèvres in the 18th century.

58. Sèvres. Cup and *trembleuse* saucer. 1766. Louvre, Paris. The decoration of this piece, so busy and intricate, and not exactly sober in taste, with its green medallions gleaming with gold inside the trellised network, might well suggest craftsmanship of a later date.

57. Sèvres. Decorated by Evans. Cup and saucer. 1762
Musée des Arts Décoratifs, Paris.

58. Sèvres. Cup and *trembleuse* saucer. 1766. Louvre, Paris.

'rose Pompadour', soft and deep at the same time, which was created in homage to the King's favourite. Rarer, but no less precious and sophisticated, were daffodil yellow, carmine, agate grey, rust red and grass green. The design known as *œil de perdrix* was often used on plain backgrounds. Decorative medallions, on a white ground, are lightly framed in gold in the form of blossoming sprigs, and the same designs are repeated along sides and bases, with handles and spouts forming a vaguely ornamental design. Flowers, more delicate than the often stately compositions of the *Deutsche Blumen*, are a dominant decorative feature. They are featured in bunches, on their own, and in the lightest of garlands, as in the costly services for Madame du Barry and for the Cardinal de Rohan (1771–1772). Many artists were employed, each one specialising in a particular genre, flowers, garlands, animals, landscapes or figures, and often they signed their work with their own initials.

Behind all the developments at Sèvres is the ever present tradition of the great French 18th century. The form of Sèvres ware is in perfect harmony with Louis XV furniture; the designs which adorn vases and services are derived from Arcadian and mythological scenes from Watteau, Boucher and Fragonard, whose work often also inspired groups of figures in biscuit. The sculptor Etienne Maurice Falconet was for a time director of the sculpture department at Sèvres, and models for the biscuit groups were derived from, and sometimes directly provided by, other great sculptors of 18th-century France, from Duplessis to Pigalle, from Lemoyne to Houdon—whose models, for example, inspired the biscuit versions of the portraits of Voltaire and Molière.

Sèvres sculpture is almost entirely in biscuit: there are Arcadian subjects, love-scenes, children's games (the famous 'Magic Lantern' from a model by Falconet is an example) and mythological subjects which Neo-classicism had not yet forced to conform to the rules of the ancients. *Pygmalion* (1763), *Leda and the Swan* (1764), and *The Bather, or Venus Anadyomene* are among Falconet's most remarkable mythological pieces.

The figures and groups from the Sèvres factory have none of Bustelli's vein of irony, of Kändler's powers of caricature, nothing of the popular violence of the Capodimonte masked figures or the stately and rhetorical relish of certain minor works of porcelain sculpture of the period. But instead Sèvres offers a whole world of soft and languid, sometimes even weary and sickly, emotions which is perfectly suited to the opaque and soft surface of biscuit. In about 1770 designers discovered the new bourgeois 'intimism', most superbly expressed in contemporary painting by Chardin. The shepherd, the *fête galante*, the languid heroes of Metastasio were gradually giving place to intimate homely groups and calm scenes of domestic contentment.

The factory declined during the French Revolution, but revived in the Imperial period, celebrating the glories of the Empire with the flamboyance of lavish gold, of stately royal blue, and of the shapes which the classical world had glorified. And nostalgically Napoleon took the Sèvres service of 1807, decorated with pictures of his far-off victories, to his exile on St Helena.

The marks of the first period of the Vincennes factory, up to the time when it received royal patronage in 1753, were two crossed 'L's, in blue. From that year onwards, a letter was added inside the triangle formed by the two 'L's, to indicate the year it left the factory, 'A' being 1753. From 1778 the letters were doubled (e.g. 1778 was 'AA') until the outbreak of revolution in 1792. From then till the Empire the pieces had various marks, the commonest being the name of the factory written in full. During the Imperial period, the sign was 'Man. Imp de Sèvres', accompanied by the year in which the piece was made.

MINOR FRENCH FACTORIES

The histories of the oldest soft porcelain factories in France during the late 17th century, at Rouen and St Cloud, have already been outlined. From the first years of the 18th century onwards other minor or very small soft porcelain factories were opened on French territory, e.g. at Passy, Paris, at Lille and at Chantilly (1725). Sceaux started production after the opening of Vincennes and Orléans.

Sèvres, on which the smaller factories modelled themselves, had little to fear from their competition. (Their porcelain was usually somewhat fragile and often defective, and could certainly not compete with that of Sèvres.) So the main French factory allowed the smaller ones to survive, except for

59. Sèvres. Plate from a service belonging to Cardinal Louis de Rohan. 1772. Louvre, Paris.

59.   Sèvres. Plate from a service belonging to Cardinal Louis de Rohan, 1772. Louvre, Paris. At Sèvres, as at other factories, the most important services were made on commission for influential people or noble families. The Cardinal de Rohan, for whom this piece was made and whose initials can be seen delicately interwoven, was the one who was the centre of numerous scandals at the court of Louis XV.

60.   Sèvres. Sugar-bowl. 1758. Musée des Arts Décoratifs, Paris. This piece is typical of the French factory. The gold-framed medallions enclose classical objects and symbols which are still interpreted with a truly 18th-century grace.

61.   Sèvres. Ewer and basin. 1865. Musée des Arts Décoratifs, Paris. Even though the modulated outline of this piece seems to evoke the quick and harmonious shapes of the true 18th century, the heavy decoration, the gaudy colours and the lavish gold recall, almost brutally, the ponderous taste of the late 19th century.

62.   Sèvres. J. F. Philippine. Vase with flower decoration. 1830. Musée des Arts Décoratifs, Paris. The classical amphora, so fashionable in the early 19th century, is enriched and weighed down, especially in the handles, and is covered abundantly in gold. Jean François Philippine specialised in floral decoration.

60

61. Sèvres. Ewer and basin. 1865. Musée des Arts Décoratifs, Paris.

62. Sèvres. J. F. Philippine Vase with flower decoration. 1830. Musée des Arts Décoratifs, Paris.

62

Strasbourg, which as the first producers of hard paste in France could offer serious competition. At the end of the 18th century and the beginning of the 19th, when hard paste had been discovered and was in common use, and when the 'privilege' granted to Sèvres had been lessened and in the end abolished, a remarkable increase of small factories took place, many being highly successful during the years of the Empire.

Their output was exclusively Neo-classical: mostly small services, lavishly gilded, and decorated with rigidly stylised designs. The most common figure decorations were classical scenes or views, medallions with portrait-busts like artificial cameos, or stylised antique symbols or else paintings of the recent French victories. Jars were in the form of amphorae, sugar-bowls were in the form of tripods or Greek kraters. The results are uneven, sometimes flat and heavy, but also sometimes remarkably harmonious and light.

Among the best known of the lesser French factories were those of the Duke of Angoulême (1780), which after the Revolution was taken over by Dihl and Guerhard, Deruelle's factory at Clignancourt (1771–1798), and various factories in Paris.

The marks of these factories are usually given as the name of the factory or its director, written in full.

ENGLISH FACTORIES

The English factories had different beginnings from the German, French and Italian ones: they were

63. Deruelle, Clignancourt. Ewer and basin. *c.*1771–1775. Sèvres Museum.

64. St Cloud. Soup-tureen. Musée des Arts Décoratifs, Paris.

65. St Cloud. Exotic figure. Musée des Arts Décoratifs, Paris.

66

63. Deruelle, Clignancourt. Ewer and basin, *c.*1771–1775. Sèvres Museum. This is one of the earliest pieces from the small Paris factory, and is decorated with a design often found on French 18th-century porcelain. Nevertheless in the sprigs, festoons and decorative design the new *Louis Seize* taste can already be seen.

64. St Cloud. Soup-tureen. Musée des Arts Décoratifs, Paris. Adapted from an old maiolica factory at the end of the 17th century, this factory produced soft paste and was famous throughout Europe before the foundation of Sèvres. Here the traditional European shape is combined with oriental designs from the early 1700s.

65. St Cloud. Exotic figure. Musée des Arts Décoratifs, Paris. This soft paste factory also achieved first-class statuettes. The colour shades have the full range and warmth typical of soft paste.

66. Bourg la Reine. Mustard-pot. 1756. Musée des Arts Décoratifs, Paris. This is a typical shape of the French 18th century. The Bourg la Reine factory was founded in the Rue de Charonne, Paris, in 1734, moved to Mennecy, and later, in 1773, to its final home.

all started by private enterprise, without influential patronage, and with purely commercial aims. It is therefore hardly surprising that it should be the Chelsea factory which provides the earliest instance of advertised sales, with a list of articles and related prices.

The English soft paste, like the French, was made from a frit, whose components vary from factory to factory. Its basis was lime and chalk, or else quartz and sand, or again soapstone and phosphate of calcium.

Little suited, because of its fragility, for everyday dishes, English porcelain is known above all through its statuettes, in a particularly delicate range of colours, which were exactly the ones that were possible on soft porcelain.

The English factories often produced ware of the highest quality, but there were no outstanding individual artists like Kändler at Meissen or Bustelli at Nymphenburg; nor was English ceramic production backed by a strong tradition, as at Sèvres. The subjects treated were the usual ones of the Rococo tradition in Continental works.

Chelsea. The earliest dated pieces of English soft paste porcelain are certain 'goat and bee' jugs from Chelsea dated 1745. This early period was, on account of the glassy translucent quality of the ware, perhaps the finest; typical products were allegorical figures such as the *Four Seasons*. From 1770 the factory was controlled by that of Derby, the result being work known as Chelsea-Derby.

Marks on Chelsea ware include the triangle of the earliest period, and the famous anchor; an anchor in

67. Plymouth. Figure of a woman. City Art Gallery, Plymouth.

68

67.   Plymouth. Figure of a woman. City Art Gallery, Plymouth. It was a Devon man, William Cookworthy (1705–1780), who first used kaolin in England. Plymouth is indeed one of the very few English factories which produced hard paste. Their soft and light modelling is characteristic of the English statuettes.

68.   Wedgwood. Vase. 1786. The Wedgwood Museum Trust, Josiah Wedgwood & Sons, Barlaston. This vase, with the white figures on a blue ground showing the Apotheosis of Homer, is very typical of the work Wedgwood was producing at this time.

69.   English. Plate. End of 18th century. Musée des Arts Décoratifs, Paris. Apart from the Neo-classical phenomenon of Wedgwood ware, true English porcelain remained faithful for a long time to the designs of European Rococo when the Continent had already completely accepted Neo-classical designs. Note in this case the flowing shape of the plate's edge, and the frames of the medallions.

69. English. Plate. End of 18th century. Musée des Arts
Décoratifs, Paris.

relief (*c.* 1750–1753), then the red anchor, finally the gold anchor from about 1758.

Bow. The finest work of the London factory of Stratford-le-Bow dates from the 1750s. It included characteristic statuettes and tableware often decorated in the oriental style or distinctive flower subjects. The marks were either an anchor or an arrow on a circle.

Derby. The factory, which claimed to be the English Meissen, was founded about 1750 and modelled its work not only on the great Saxon factory but also on its English rival of Chelsea. Derby ware can often be distinguished by the characteristic discoloration on the base of the pieces. In 1770 the factory took over the Chelsea works, the last fine period being that of Crown Derby in the first decade of the 19th century.

Worcester. The factory, originally founded in Bristol, moved to Worcester about 1751. The ware was usually of finest quality but the design highly derivative, drawing on Chinese, English, Meissen or Sèvres work. One mark imitated a Chinese ideogram.

Plymouth. The first English true hard paste porcelain was produced here in 1768, after twenty years of experiment, by William Cookworthy. Soon afterwards the factory moved to Bristol, where the best work was produced, and in 1781 the patent was bought by a group of Staffordshire potters based on New Hall.

Other centres of English soft paste porcelain included the following: Longton Hall, flourishing during the 1750s, Lowestoft, flourishing during the latter half of the century and, like some other English factories, using a paste containing bone ash, Coalport, also sometimes called Coalbrookdale, and Swansea, producing fine porcelain in the early 19th century, much of which was bought by London firms unfinished, and then decorated.

Wedgwood, the most famous name in English ceramics, produced no true porcelain, but the impact of his improved cheap cream earthenware, often decorated by transfer-print, and his full-scale application of industrial methods to the pottery business had repercussions on all aspects of the trade throughout Europe, while his black basaltes (or 'black porcelain') and jasperwares enjoyed a considerable vogue in their own right. His mark was the name 'Wedgwood' imprinted in full in the porcelain.

OTHER EUROPEAN FACTORIES

Founded by private enterprise, the two Swiss factories—at Zürich (1765, hard paste, mark 'Z') and at Nyon (1781–1813, soft paste, mark a fish) took their shapes and decoration from Germany and France.

Holland, which had been ahead of other countries in its appreciation of oriental porcelain, and which boasted an ancient ceramic tradition, nevertheless had no factories of any great importance. Most Dutch factories had been founded by private enterprise during the second half of the century, and were mainly influenced by France. Among the best known, the one at Weesp was founded in 1764, moved to Oude Loosdrecht, then to Oude Amstel and finally closed in 1819. Its marks: two crossed swords, surrounded by three dots and the initials 'M.o L.' with an asterisk. There was also the factory at The Hague (1775–1784) whose mark was a stork with a fish in its mouth.

In Belgium the best known factory was the one at Tournai, founded in 1753 (mark: a tower), which mainly produced groups and figures in soft porcelain; artisans from the French factories at Mennecy and Sèvres and the English Chelsea factory worked there.

The Copenhagen factory, after its first unsuccessful attempts in the first half of the 18th century, started production in 1755, when kaolin was discovered on Danish soil. In 1779 the factory was acquired by the state, and its best period began. Its most famous piece is the service known as 'Flora Danica' (about 1790), decorated, in honour of the revival of scientific interests in the late 18th century, with the flowers and plants of Denmark, reproduced with the accuracy of a scientific illustration. The Danish factory's mark was a cursive 'F' and a '5' (Frederick V) until 1766, and after that three waves.

The Danish factory which functioned on the island of Marieberg was of little importance. Its mark was 'MB', surmounted by three crowns in a line. It had a chequered career from 1758 to 1788.

The Russian factory at St Petersburg, founded in 1744—whose leading light was once again the deserter Hunger—made its chief headway under Catherine II (1762–1796). The shapes and decorative designs were derived from German and French factories, although the output was somewhat limited. The marks are the initials of the various monarchs.

LIST OF ILLUSTRATIONS   Page